CONTENTS

DISCLAIMER

INTRODUCTION

Effectively managing a restaurant is not an easy task. It requires that you, as a restaurant owner, pay attention to various aspects of your business to be able to succeed. However challenging it may be, owning a restaurant is a dream of many; it is, unarguably, among one of the most rewarding businesses a person can run.

No matter how much effort you've put into running your restaurant, there's always room for enhancement. It is surprising to see that even the slightest of improvements can yield great results when it comes to increasing your customer base.

Among the most important principles of running a restaurant is proper leadership and organizational skills. Good leadership skills will determine how well you train your staff to excel at providing nothing but the very best customer service possible.

On the other hand, your organizational skills as a restaurant owner will exemplify how well you manage and adapt to changing circumstances. Some of the most important aspects in this regard include creating an alluring ambience of your restaurant to draw more customers and in order to offer them a comfortable experience of dining at your place.

However, without proper marketing and advertising techniques, it would be hard for you to have your name heard amidst cutting-edge competition in the hospitality industry. Today's social media has allowed business owners to expand their reach in extremely interesting and addictive ways.

It is also of an utmost importance that you keep up with the ever-changing needs of your customers. What counts is your passion to serve exemplary dishes with exceptional service which is certain to put a smile on the face of your customers. Whatever your target market, you must have a well-laid business strategy that is open for any amendments and improvements on your road to perfection.

This book is written in order to help you boost your sales and expand your customer base. From redesigning your menu to carrying out a comprehensive advertising campaign – we have included 50 ways through which you can grow your business at unprecedented rates.

1 IMPROVING THE AMBIENCE

The importance and necessity of having a good ambience at a restaurant cannot be undermined. Naturally, the more comfortable and attractive your restaurant is, the more people it will attract. You should take the essential steps to ensure that whatever the theme of your restaurant, it should be visually appealing and comfortable.

1.1 Understand Your Target Market

The first thing you should be clear on is your target market. What type of target audience are you planning to serve? Are they teenagers mostly? Business professionals? Or families?

This is important, as it will help you in making the right decisions for when it comes to the designing part. If, for example, your restaurant is located in the heart of a business district, then you'll be expecting a lot of business people as your customers. You need to understand their needs and expectations. Therefore, in such a situation, an elegantly designed restaurant would do the trick.

There's a strong link between figuring out your target audience, and then marketing your restaurant appropriately. One of the major mistakes restaurant owners make is to try to make their restaurant appeal to everyone. So if you have similar ideas, as in if you believe your target market includes everyone – you should change that now!

There's a difference between what *target market* is, and what it isn't. You need to be clear on this:

A target market is that portion of population that is very likely to become your customers.

That being said, here are a few things you need to ponder upon:

1. Figure out what kinds of things people will enjoy based on the surroundings of your restaurant. Consider the gender, age, race, religion, income and background of the population you intend to serve.
2. While not directly linked to the ambience, but because you would already be doing the research – try to find out what medium of communication is common among these people so that you would be able to utilize it to the fullest for marketing purposes.

1.2 Install the Ideal Flooring

The flooring of your restaurant will be among one of the most important in making the ambience more appealing and comfortable. Depending on the theme of your restaurant, you could choose the flooring from the numerous options, such as tiles, laminate floors as well as carpets.

Restaurants are high traffic areas, meaning that throughout the day and night, people will be coming and going, so keep this into consideration when choosing the type of flooring.

Here are a few factors which you will need to consider when making the right choice for your restaurant flooring:

- The Aesthetics
- The Acoustics
- Ease of Maintenance of Flooring

Every restaurant is unique; you need to understand the traffic pattern of yours. Consider how guests and the servers will move around the restaurant. Which areas would be exposed to the greatest traffic?

It is also wise to consider how your customers will be dressed. This generally doesn't matter much, until fine-dining restaurants are considered. Here, you will have customers wearing sharp stiletto heels that will exert quite a bit of a force on your floor.

If on the other hand, you have a restaurant on a beach or anywhere nearby – then expect lots of sand, scores of flip-flops and maybe some dripping salt water!

Review your cleaning methods too. How do you plan on dealing with spills and food droppings? If your restaurant caters for families, then you should expect lots of spills – avoid carpets at all costs.

1·3 Get the Lighting Right

The ambience, by definition, is 'the character and atmosphere of a place'. This atmosphere is affected by several factors, one of the major players being the lighting. Lighting sets the right mood, and breathes in a soul into the environment.

To give your restaurant an elegant touch, use spotlights to shine upon menu boards, on art pieces or any paintings. You could also incorporate dimmer switches to adjust the intensity of lights to suit the time of the day or night. Also make sure that the lighting is spread evenly throughout the dining area of your restaurant.

Don't neglect the outdoor lighting either! These lights will give the first impression of your restaurant.

Lighting Guidelines

Various levels of lighting are suited for different meals during day and night. Here are some general guidelines to help you choose the appropriate intensity of lights depending on the operating timings of your restaurant.

Breakfast: A lot of light should be available so that your customers can read newspapers while eating.

Lunch: For a fast food restaurant, moderate intensity lighting would suffice. It will also help in bringing about fast turnover of your customers that are needed especially during rush hours.

Dinner: For dinner, low intensity lighting is suitable as it creates a comfortable and intimate atmosphere.

Fine-Dining: Lighting should be perfect in fine-dining restaurants. Similar to the lighting for dinner, the lighting at a fine-dining restaurant should be of a low intensity in order to make the atmosphere more intimate.

Themed Restaurants: If you have a restaurant that features a particular theme, you should use lighting that complements the theme and makes it more appealing.

Look around, you're sure to find a lot of options suitable for your restaurant.

1.4 Tune the Sounds

Sound isn't just about what tracks you should play. It's related to each and every little sound in your restaurant, from the kitchen, from people's conversations and even the sound of any equipment in your restaurant. All of these things can contribute to background noise and

spoil the ambience – no one likes a noisy restaurant!

Nevertheless, it is the target audience that determines how much you should attempt to control the noise. For a family restaurant, the noise may in fact be beneficial to give off an aura of busyness. While for a more elegant setting, say a restaurant which is usually visited by couples only, you may want to try to dampen the sounds by installing a carpet as well as by taking other measures to make the ambience a little more romantic.

1.5 Use Colors Wisely

Choose you colors based on your theme. This color should match the furniture, rather than making the whole setting feel out of place. For a fine dining restaurant, stick with lighter shades to portray an elegant look.

For a fast food eating place, you can enjoy the liberty of experimenting with intense colors and vivid shades.

When it comes to choosing the colors for your restaurant, as long as you avoid the following, everything would apparently work out fine.

What to Avoid

In a restaurant where there will be a lot of children, it is inadvisable to use lighter shades on the wall. The level which may be touched by children will tend to stain quickly, thus spoiling the looks.

Avoid using a neutral tone along with another tone that is also neutral. This will give your restaurant a dull look.

Avoid primary colors unless or until you want to put off adults. Use of primary colors is only suitable for those restaurants that expect a lot of children. For adults, it can generally be a turn off as it would make your restaurant look childish.

1·6 Take Care of Ventilation

Regardless of the size of your restaurant, you should pay attention to proper ventilation. The last thing customers want while eating is to feel as if they are suffocating in a closed box and that too with unpleasant odors!

Small-sized restaurants do need to pay more attention to ventilation issues.

Here are a few advantages that you can benefit from as a result of good ventilation:

Improved Air Quality: A commercial kitchen can produce quite a few harmful gases and other substances. For the safety of not only the customers, but also your staff, a ventilation system should be installed so that these gases can be expelled out.

Reduction of Heat Levels: The heat in a kitchen can make it unbearable for the workers to tolerate – if your workers get exhausted, the quality of the food may begin to decline.

1·7 Create an Alluring Décor

Flooring, lighting and sounds – all contribute towards the décor. Apart from these factors, the furniture you use, and the fittings you install in your rest rooms – all count towards improving or degrading a décor.

Regardless of the type of restaurant you run, stick to quality. Customers do notice these things in detail, and an appealing décor can do wonders when it comes to increasing your sales.

1·8 Decorate Appropriately

Decorate your restaurant appropriate to your planned theme. Hang paintings, place pieces of art that go well with the reminiscent of the types of cuisine you offer. Figure the perfect ways to accent your tabletops – the possibilities are endless, let your imagination run wild!

1·9 Keep it Clean!

Even if you have the best ambience in town along with the finest food, if your restaurant lags behind in cleanliness, you'll lose customers. You need to make sure that any food droppings or spills are looked after immediately, without them lying around for customers to see. This gives a bad impression, and bad news travels fast!

1·10 Take Care of the Temperature

It may be below freezing outside with snow everywhere; or it may be so hot that the mercury might be shooting up the scale – but this shouldn't concern your customers. Once they have entered your restaurant, they should be welcomed by comfortable temperature levels.

That being said, you should take measures in order to keep a well-maintained temperature, regardless of what's happening outdoors. 70 degrees Fahrenheit is usually considered to provide a comfortable environment.

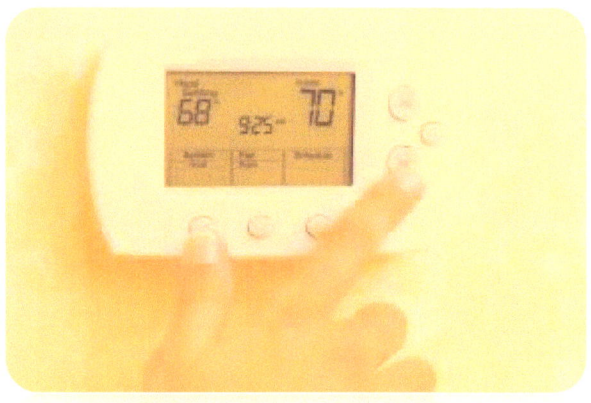

2 REACHING OUT EFFECTIVELY

A well-planned marketing strategy plays a significant role in reaching out and grabbing the attention of potential customers. While traditional marketing is always an option, great emphasis should be given to the numerous potential of Internet as a marketing platform.

2.1 Remain Up to Date

As a restaurant owner, you should be aware of the ongoing trends in restaurant marketing. Keep yourself apprised of statistics along with facts and figures, as this will greatly help you in coming up with an effective marketing plan for your restaurant.

This is more of a necessity than a luxury, as competition reaches at its peak in the hospitality industry; you'll need to remain on your toes.

2.2 Create a Website

Scores of people search the internet for places where they can dine.

If you don't have a presence on the internet, then you don't exist for them.

Have a fully functional website that will establish an awareness of your business' existence. Also, you want people to reach your website before they reach your competitor's. To achieve this, you'll have to expand your presence and ranking on the internet using search-engine optimization techniques.

To be called fully functional, your website should at least contain the following sections:

◉ **Your Restaurant's Location Along With A Map**

Integrating a Google Map onto your website is the best way to do this. A lot of people search for eating places using their mobile phones, a map will help them locate you.

◉ **Provide Contact Information**

You should ensure that contact details such as e-mail addresses, telephone numbers or any other information that will allow customers to get in touch with you are posted on the website.

◉ **Display Pictures**

You should have several high quality pictures taken and put up on your website. Your pictures tell potential customers a lot about your restaurant. These could be of the exterior of the restaurant (showing your restaurant's façade), interior setting as well as of the food and drinks that you serve.

Always Include Your Menu

It is surprising to see that quite a few restaurants do not post their menus online, for whatever the reason. While few that do, sometimes fail to keep them up to date. It gives off a really bad impression if there are

differences in the menus found at your website and the restaurant – and embarrassing too if a customer points it out.

Why not go a step ahead and add the nutritional values of each of your servings – many people are interested in learning about the nutritional values of food that they eat.

Include Some Information About Your Chef

Your chef is a very important player in the running of your restaurant. Give him or her some credit and post interesting information about them. You would be surprised how many people will be asking for the chef to thank him for the wonderful food!

◉ Add a Blog Section

In today's internet-savvy world, a blog page is necessary to get your rankings right in search engines. You could have engaging content created, anything related to the food industry and the cuisines that you serve!

◉ Online Reservation Tool

This is not necessary for each and every type of restaurant. However, your fine-dining restaurant would do better than just 'fine' if you let your customers reserve tables conveniently through the website.

2.3 Engage in SEO Practices

SEO or Search Engine Optimization is simply a way to increase your rating in search engines such as Google. The aim is to make sure your restaurant lists in the top results whenever a person searches for anything related to food in your area.

Gone are the days when only large businesses utilized these techniques, more and more smaller businesses and start-ups are now realizing the need of implementing SEO practices in their internet marketing strategy.

2.4 Keep an Eye on Review Sites

It is the reputation of a place that can make the difference between success and failure. There are a number of review sites on the internet where people post their experiences after trying out a new restaurant or diner.

Frequently visit these sites to learn what people have to say about your restaurant. Use any negative comments as a tool to correct those complaints and improve your service. This will enhance your relation with your customers, as they will feel that their opinion is respected.

2.5 Make Use of Restaurant Reservation Tools Online

You can use a website like OpenTable to make it convenient for people to make a reservation from the comfort of their homes, without even dialing a number. If you have your own website –which you should- then you should also consider providing a means to make a reservation from your own website.

Just a few clicks is all it takes.

2.6 Reach Out on Social Media

Social Media offers an excellent way for businesses to interact with their customers and leads. Create a page on Facebook and keep your customers in the loop regarding latest developments and offers at your restaurant. You could also *tweet* regularly with news and interesting facts to keep your followers hooked up.

Give people a reason for following you on social media. You can consider providing random discount offers to those who follow your restaurant's page.

LinkedIn is another platform useful for building professional relationships with others in the same industry.

Here are the things you can do using social media websites:

1. Gets feedback on your services, quality of food and events.
2. Promote any new additions to your menu.
3. Invite new people with special offers and discounts which they cannot refuse.
4. Engage in direct conversations with your current as well as potential customers.
5. Increase your business' awareness by offering exciting giveaways.
6. Meet new business partners
7. Find new employees.
8. Continuously keep an eye on your restaurant's reputation as well as resolving any complaints.

2.7 Establish a Customer Loyalty Program

A customer loyalty program is a great way to keep customers coming back for more. You can send newsletters both in email and by post

that can include coupons, special deals and offers for your loyal customers.

You should be aware of that customer loyalty programs do not work as well with each and every type of restaurant. For example, loyalty programs actually tend to bring down the value of expensive fine-dining restaurants. This is because the people that dine here can afford the costs and usually do not worry about getting discounts. The same goes for luxurious establishments. For those restaurants that cater to tourists, a loyalty program would rarely benefit them.

On the other hand, neighborhood restaurants that tend to get quite a bit of customers who come in for breakfast or lunch do well with customer loyalty programs.

2.8 Consider Marketing Using Email

When compared to direct marketing, email marketing has proven its worth. Email is a more efficient and environmental friendly way to get in touch with your customers, so you'll not only be benefitting your business, but you'll also be protecting the environment.

2.9 Invite Local Food Bloggers

You can also invite local food bloggers and treat them to your cuisine. These bloggers can then write reviews for you that can help improve your search engine rankings. Their feedback will also help in portraying a positive reputation.

2.10 Be Patient

Don't expect to see immediate results. It can take time before your restaurant even starts to show up in the initial pages of search engines. Also, it would be impractical to immediately expect a lot of followers on your social media pages – give these things time and they will begin to settle in as you want them to. Just be consistent with your endeavor.

3 REFINING CUSTOMER SERVICE

Restaurants fall under the category of the hospitality industry; and the hospitality industry is all about serving the customer. You can have the best food with the perfect ambience, yet you will see a sharp decline in your business if you lag behind in providing a refined customer service. Here are a few tips to help you improve your customer services and make your customers feel privileged and valued.

3.1 Create a Strategy

Unless or until you, as the owner of the restaurant, are clear about how you plan on providing services to your customers, you will be unable to instruct and train your managers and staff. Sit down and take your time to develop a well-laid plan – ensuring that you include each and every bit of detail of what you plan to accomplish. Consider each and every aspect from the point the customers walk into your restaurant, to the point when they are leaving after having the meal.

Here are a few things that would give you an idea of what your strategy should cover:

1. How can you seat your customers quickly, without them having to wait?
2. How quickly can you serve them their orders? Can you aim to achieve a fixed service time?
3. How many tables should a single staff attend to?
4. What are the ways in which the staff can become more friendly and welcoming?

These types of questions will help you figure out where your customer service is headed, and where it should be.

Your strategy should also have details on how your staff should interact with you customers, taking the following aspects under consideration:

Listening Skills

Those staff that is responsible for interacting directly with the customers should possess excellent listening skills. They should listen with the goal of comprehension without interrupting or cutting short customers while they are speaking.

Asking Skills

Asking the right questions in the right manner is essential for keeping customers happy. Good questions can help uncover the needs and requirements of customers. The tone of the staff should be friendly and polite.

For example, rather than bluntly asking "Rare or medium?" when a customer is placing an order for a steak, it would be far more polite and appropriate to wait until the customer has finished speaking; only then the question should be put forward, and that too in a way that is more engaging, such as "Would you like your so-and-so steak as rare, medium or well-done?"

Responsibility

A sense of responsibility should prevail among all of your staff. They should be aware of the fact that the way they attend to customers, the type of service they provide to them and the attitude which they have with them determines the reactions of a customer.

A lack of responsibility will only deteriorate customer service.

Knowledge and Responsiveness

If your staff has the awareness and thorough knowledge of what's on the menu and what individual dishes have in them – be assured that your customers will be impressed, to say the least. Quite often, customers ask a server of what they can expect in a specific dish – only to find out that the servers themselves are not clear. Your strategy should include training sessions for the staff in order to get them acquainted with the cuisine your restaurant serves.

Accuracy and Timing

Among other things, accuracy of taking orders and serving them with the right timing is essential. The last thing you would want is serving your customer something other than what he or she ordered – bad customer service and bad customer retention!

3·2 Meet Your Staff

Once you have a detailed strategy on your hands, the next thing you should do is convey that to your staff. After all, they are the ones who would be representing your restaurant.

You should clearly assign your staff their individual goals and responsibilities by sharing the customer service strategy. This meeting is important, as you want consistency among your staff so that each time a customer visits your restaurant, they get the same type of service every time.

3·3 Take a Walk

When was the last time you actually interacted with one of your customers? Yes, they are *your* customers – and you should set an example for your staff by walking around the floor once in a while.

Approach your customers and ask them about their experience at your place. Did they enjoy it? How are they finding the food? Are the desserts up to their standards? While you're there, why not take along a free refill to surprise your customers.

These kinds of acts can do wonders in spreading good word about your restaurant. Not only will you be securing your current customers, but also indirectly inviting others to have an experience the wonderful customer service.

If you get any complaints from your customers, make it up to them with a complimentary drink or dessert. This way, you'll not only calm them down, but you may also avoid losing a customer.

All of this will show your customers how much you appreciate their business. Customer appreciation can go a long way in retaining your customers as well as inviting new ones through great reputation.

3.4 Consider Becoming a Child-Friendly Restaurant

By implementing several changes, you can become a child-friendly restaurant. Families *always* prefer to dine out at these restaurants as it makes it easier for the parents to deal with the children and keep them engaged with quite a few interesting things that such places have to offer.

To become a child-friendly restaurant, you should consider implementing the following:

Set Up a Cheerful Décor

As we previously discussed in Chapter 1, the décor is among the very first of the things that customers notice. A cheerful décor with vibrant, alluring colors would act as an inviting signal for children and their parents alike. Also, to make cleaning easy, consider getting leather and vinyl furnishings and beautiful tiles instead of carpets.

Include Offerings for Children on Your Menu

A serving of lamb rump with baby beets might not be too appealing for children. Add some interesting additions to your menu to accommodate your young customers.

Consider printing a separate menu for children to make it more attractive for them. Children love to choose things for themselves.

Include Appropriate Seating for Children

Make it easy for both the children and the parents to enjoy their meals by providing appropriate seating arrangements for children. High chairs and booster seats for the little ones is an investment that will prove worthwhile!

Introduce Activities for Kids and Make it Special for Them

Handout coloring books along with crayons for children while they wait for the food to arrive; small toys are also a great option.

Surprise the children by making them feel special. This could be as easy as getting your chef to write the children's names onto their plates using chocolate sauce!

Spread the Word

Whenever you make the changes – spread the word about it! Why not consider handing out baseball caps to kids with the name of your restaurant on it? During the promotion period, you can also consider handing out anything from t-shirts to story books and even toys!

Carry Out the Necessary Adjustments in Restrooms

When you expect children, you should also expect diapers that need changing! Make appropriate changes to your rest rooms by providing changing tables.

3.5 Improve Standards of Cleanliness

You cannot deny the fact that people love to visit cleaner restaurants, as compared to their less-immaculate counterparts. You should take every measure possible to avoid situations that would otherwise turn away your customers.

Cleanliness is not limited just to the expensive restaurants – it applies to each and every type of eatery out there!

Check Your Restrooms

If a customer finds a restroom to be dirty, they would gain an impression that the restaurant is incompetent. The cleanliness of the restrooms should be checked at regular intervals throughout the time the restaurant is open. The frequency should be increased during rush hours. Another thing is to make sure that enough supply of toilet paper, soup and any other toiletries are available.

Groom the Servers

It is the servers that come in direct contact with the customers as they bring food to the table. You must set standards of hygiene that the servers must abide by. Give off a good image when it comes to hygiene of your restaurant!

Keep Tables Spotless

Any spills or food droppings on the tables should never be left lying around. This is among one of the worst things that you could do to spoil your reputation.

3.6 Serve Food As It Should Be Served

Unless your menu says about a particular food that it should be served at room temperature, always make sure the food is being served hot. Except where it is supposed to be like that, food served at room temperature only implies that it was left out for sometime before being served.

Besides serving food at the proper temperature, make sure it is served along with the relevant bells and whistles. If your char-grilled burger is supposed to be served with an extra fries and a free drink – make sure these things are served accordingly without having the customer to ask for it.

3.7 Maintain Consistency

One of the greatest challenges that restaurants face is maintaining a consistent standard of service. A restaurant creates numerous types of dishes each day, week after week and for years to come. The menu may not be changing, but the one thing that is extremely prone to vary is the standard.

The standard of not only the dishes, but also the customer service is of a paramount importance. The success of a restaurant depends on this. As the word spreads about how delicious your food is, you need to be able to treat your new customers with exactly the same standard of food that they had heard about.

Take a moment to think about this. One of the greatest expenses of a new restaurant is due to the mass marketing advertisements that it carries out in an attempt to draw new customers. The next step involves turning these new customers into *repeat* customers by providing quality food and service.

Some restaurant owners, in a bid to get more of the new customers, fail to observe that their standards of service have begun to decline. This decline in quality will have two major effects:

- New Customers will not become repeat customers (and they will spread the word, for sure!)
- You will begin to lose your repeat customers. This is because they would be the first ones to notice a decline in the standard of service.

Once this starts to happen, it will become a mammoth of a task to secure clients and generate a source of income.

This is why it's vital that you take measures to **maintain the consistency of your food and service at all times**.

Following are some ways that will help you maintain consistency throughout the years.

1. Operate Within The Legal Outline

It is obligatory for any business to operate within the legal policies of any country. This helps in ensuring that all businesses are steadfast on the laid down safety standards.

This is especially important for businesses in the hospitality industry where food is involved.

When a restaurant owner strictly follows the guidelines set by governing authorities, he or she not only guarantees that the food is safe and of a good quality, but also helps the restaurant maintain consistency by achieving such targets.

2. Servings Must Be Consistent

Keeping the servings consistent each and every time portrays a positive image of your restaurant's management to the customer. The last thing you would want is food portions fluctuating in both size and quantity.

Apart from its obvious benefits, consistent servings will also help you keep a track on your *Restaurant Portion Control*.

For those who aren't aware of what Restaurant Portion Control is:

The Restaurant Portion Control is the process of keeping track on the portions coming out of the kitchen in order to keep the food cost in check.

3. Service Must be Consistent

A consistent staff that meets and greets each and every customer in the same, professional and refined manner is vital for crossing any success barriers!

Also, when it comes to serving the customers at the table, consistency and efficiency go hand in hand to make the customer feel valued.

3·8 Avoid Common Social Media Mistakes

We discussed how important it is to utilize the social media in order to fill up your restaurant's seats in Chapter 2 of this book (2.6).

Social media is undoubtedly the key to establishing an online presence, maintaining clients and for gaining new ones. That being said, if used incorrectly, social media can do more bad than good. This is why it is important that you avoid the following social media mistakes that many entrepreneurs make:

1. Mixing Personal Life and Business

While there is absolutely nothing wrong with using social media networks such as Facebook and Twitter to pursue your personal interests. The problem arises when people start using their business accounts for personal purposes.

This could confuse your followers, especially if you post any content that nothing to do with your business. Confusion is one thing, on a serious note – they may even stop following you!

2. Not Posting Regularly

One basic rule of using social media is that you have to stay current – and keep your followers current too! There is really no point in having a social media page which you created to promote your business, if you do not post regularly.

A stagnant page is good for nothing and will not keep your followers interested in what your business has to offer, let alone attract new ones.

Post content regularly that is **related** to your restaurant; this can include interesting information about the type of cuisine you serve, and if your restaurant serves a foreign cuisine – why not post interesting information about the culture of that place?

3. Posting Too Much

Just the way not posting regularly is harmful for your business, so is posting too frequently. It certainly is great to see your business' page active, but too much activity is actually known to cut down on the number of seats that you fill up!

The principle is same as TV commercials; the more you see the same commercial, you tend to grow bored of it.

4. Not Responding

Social media is about getting in touch with the public. You need to make sure that your followers feel as if they are being valued, if you're to get them into your restaurant.

Some people will post questions onto your website – answer them, even if the answer seems obvious.

Some people may even post negative feedback onto your page regarding their experience at your place. Take this feedback in a constructive way, attend to them and inform them that you regret that they had a bad experience – and try to make them an offer in order to gain their trust. This will really help you outshine your competition!

3.9   Provide Comment Cards

Providing your customers a comment card after they have had the meal is an exceptional way of getting their feedback. Many restaurant owners do not realize the importance of a comment card. It isn't only a way of getting feedback out of the customers, but it can also help your business in the following ways:

It can help build better customer relations

Customer cards send out a message to the customers that their feedback is valued and that they are welcome to express any opinions or suggestions which they may have. In essence, it's a way of showing that you care about your customers.

This tends to create a bond of trust between the service provider (you) and the customer – and may well be the reason for a customer becoming a repeat client!

Gather Marketing Information

A customer card also provides a way to capture valuable information about the particular audience who visit your restaurant. You can then utilize this data for launching targeted marketing campaigns that will definitely succeed. Simply put, the more information you have regarding your customers, you will be equipped to serve them much better ways.

They Provide a Means of Venting Out

Never underestimate the power of an unhappy customer. News, especially bad ones, travels faster than the speed of light. By providing your customers with a comment card, you are offering them a means to vent out their experience onto the card. Now can offer you two benefits; firstly, the customer may not spread the word to friends and family after writing the comments (because they vented out their emotions). Secondly, you'll have some feedback that would require pondering upon in order to avoid any unhappy customers in the future.

How to Implement a Customer Feedback System

Comment cards are an integral part of a customer feedback system in that they provide a great opportunity for customers to give their opinion regarding food quality, service, ambience and cleanliness among other things.

Follow these guidelines when implementing comment cards into the feedback system:

Utilize Professional Printing Services

In order to have your comment cards taken seriously, you have to ensure that they carry a professional look. Utilize the services of a professional printer to have the cards designed and printed in an appropriate style that suits your restaurant's theme.

Be Concise

The language you use on the card should be simple and concise without creating any kind of confusion among your customers.

Whatever questions you ask, make sure they are to the point. Remember that you are not creating a large survey, but just a comment card.

Place the Cards at the Proper Location

You need to make sure that you place the comment cards at a place that is easily accessible and in full view of the customers so that they can reach out and pick one.

You could also have your servers deliver a card for each table along with the bill.

Make Returning the Cards Easy

Make it easy for the customers to return the filled-out comment card either by providing a drop box or by offering to collect them after they've finished their meal.

3·10 Know Ways of Dealing with Disruptive Customers

As a restaurant owner, you will have to face disruptive customers every now and then. This could be due to a number of reasons and it is essential that you learn ways on how to go about dealing with such clients. The major problems arise when a customer starts acting up under the influence of alcohol.

If you serve alcohol at your restaurant, or are planning to do so, you should be thoroughly aware of the following guidelines:

As soon as you notice that a customer is starting to show symptoms of being drunk, the first thing that needs to be done is to stop serving them. Also, if a person who is already under the influence of alcohol enters your eatery – you should also refuse to serve them. On hearing this, they may label this act as being illegal – do not pay heed to this claim, as this is a perfectly responsible way of dealing with such situations.

If the customer was being served in your restaurant, then you should stop serving any alcoholic beverages. On the contrary, offer them a cup of coffee or another non-alcoholic drink.

Call a taxi for your customer when it is time for them to leave. They will insist, but assure them that it is safe for them to go home in a taxi and they are welcome to drop by later to take their car. Be a responsible citizen, and do not let them drive.

If the customer starts to lose his or her temper, or starts to act in an unacceptable manner, have them escorted out of the restaurant and the police should be called. You wouldn't want to create a scene inside your restaurant.

Train Your Staff

Restaurant owners are responsible for ensuring that alcohol is sold in a controlled manner. Those restaurants that serve these beverages should have staff that is well trained to handle such situations. TIPS, or Training for Intervention Procedures, is a specialized program designed for restaurant staff. It trains them and offers them valuable advice on how to identify a person who might have consumed alcohol in great quantities. It also provides guidelines on how to deal with such people in the best way possible.

For more information about the TIPS, visit its website at www.gettips.com.

 **ENHANCING THE MENU**

A menu can be a powerful tool to help you boost your sales. It is a critical component for a restaurant's success provided that it is designed in a manner that takes every little advantage of the *psychology of menus*. As the owner of a restaurant, it is important that you understand how a menu can affect your customer's selection. It is estimated that customers spend an average of 109 seconds in going through the menu – not a lot of time, is it?

This lack of time means that you need to have a well designed menu that does justice to whatever you have in house to offer. From mouthwatering cuisine to exotic drinks – each and every item should be portrayed in the best possible manner.

You may not be aware that there actually is a field of study that aims at figuring out the intricacies of constructing a menu, it is called *menu engineering;* or more commonly as Menu Psychology.

4.1 Understand Menu Psychology

Regardless of the type of restaurant you run, the menu can have some surprising effects. By claiming that you have a good menu, you shouldn't only be referring to how good the food is, but you should say it in a more literal way. Menu psychology can help you design the perfect menu for your place. Before you dig into designing it, you need to understand a few things first.\

According to menu psychology, menu items are divided into four distinct categories; and no, they are not appetizers, refreshments, main course and desserts! They are divided as follows:

- **Stars** – The *Stars* consist of those items that are extremely popular and they also offer high rates of profitability. The ultimate aim of every restaurant owner should be to sell as much of the *Stars* as possible to ensure maximum revenue is being generated.
- **Plow Horse** – A *Plow Horse* consists of those items on the menu which are also high on their popularity but generate low profits. Such items are generally placed in hard to see locations on the menu as the kind of revenue they generate is not impressive to say the least.
- **Dogs** – The dogs are those dishes or items that are neither popular, nor do they generate a good profit. These types of items should be revamped in order to reach them the level of a *Plow Horse,* or better yet, the *Stars*. On the other hand, if this is not possible, then consider wiping them off your menu for good.
- **Puzzles** – These items may not be as popular, but they definitely generate a great amount of revenue. The aim of a restaurant owner should be to find ways to sell more of these.

So how should you go about managing these four items? Well, to start with, your first target would be to increase the number of ***stars***, while you try to minimize or completely eliminate the ***plow horses.*** The ***puzzles*** should be placed on the menu in a manner that would have them stand out and grab attention, while the ***dogs*** can be sent to the docks.

4.2 Locate the Sweet Spot

The *sweet spot* of a menu is that portion where you should place those items that get you the maximum profit. The menu's sweet spot is used by restaurants in an attempt to make certain items stand out and be noticed.

The question is, how can you determine the sweet spot on the menu? To understand this, you will need to absorb a little bit of psychology first:

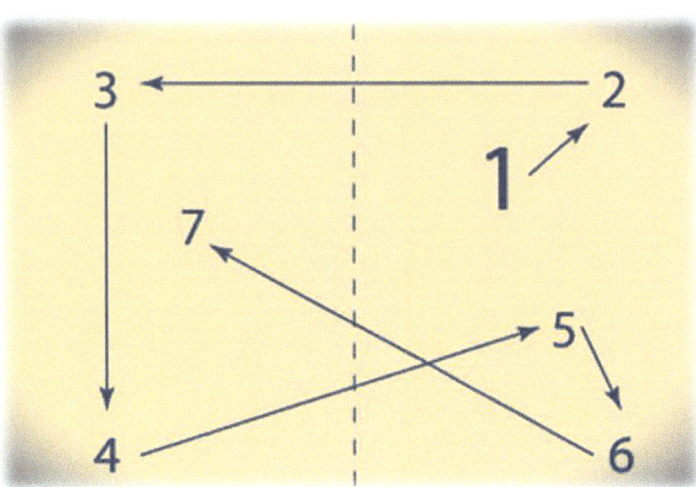

The Serial Position Effect

How people go about remembering things can be defined by the Serial Position Effect. There are two ways through which people remember – namely the *Recency Effect* and the *Primacy Effect*.

Primacy Effect: According to the Primacy Effect, there is a greater chance that items that are on the top of a list are more likely to be remembered as compared to those that are at the bottom. For example, if you have a long list (of anything, grocery items, things to do etc) and you are repeating it in order to memorize it – those items that are on the top will have more time to get transferred from the short-term memory to the long-term memory as you may have repeated them more often than other items down the list.

Recency Effect: On the contrary, according to the Recency Effect, those items that are at the bottom of a list are more likely to be remembered because those were the read by you only recently.

Now, you may be wondering what these things have to do with a restaurant menu. A restaurant menu is essentially a list, and what you should do is place the most profitable items on the top *and* bottom portions of your list – thus benefiting from both the Primacy and Recency Effects. That will be your sweet spot.

4.3 Consider How People Scan the Menu

Another aspect that should be considered while designing the menu is the way people *scan* through the menu. If you recall, people only spend around 108 seconds on a menu. They do not *read*, rather they *skim* through it.

This makes it necessary that during the designing of the menu, you consider how people scan.

According to research, it is believed that on a two-panel menu, people start off by going through the **top-right** portion; then they cross over to the **top-left.** After going through the list on the on the left, they cross over back to the right side of the menu, fixing their eyes approximately somewhere close to the **middle** of the page.

You need to understand that there is no hard and fast rule that can determine the exact scanning pattern of the customers. Every person is different, and they will go through the menu in different ways. Nevertheless, based on the general scan patterns, you can design your menu based on the *Serial Position Effect* you learned about on the previous page.

Don't forget to add color – vibrant images of food and drink can have a powerful effect on the mind, why not benefit from it?

4.4 Add Subtle Cues

Another great way of taking advantage of psychological persuasion techniques is by adding subtle cues to the menu. These cues can help you sell those dishes that may not be as popular, but generate great profit (*puzzle, see 4.1*).

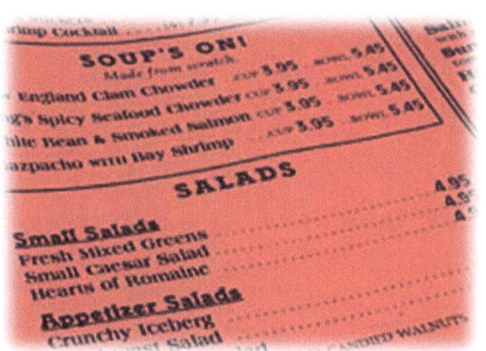

You can try out the following and see how good they turn out for you:

Eliminate the Dollar Sign – According to research, customers spend more money when the prices on a menu card are not accompanied by the dollar sign. The figure of $14.99 will make customers more aware of the cost than when the price is listed as being 14.99 without the dollar sign.

Avoid the Pennies – The pennies can actually make the customers become more aware of the money they are spending. There is really no point in listing a price as $24.99 when you can round of at $25 – the customers *know* they aren't saving much with a penny. However, there's nothing wrong with using them where strong psychology can kick in; for example, customers may feel a big difference in $1.99 and $2.00, whereas it's a difference of just a penny!

4.5 Write Suggestive Descriptions

Descriptions of what's on the menu are important as it tells the customer what to expect in that particular dish. A good description is one that can grab a customer's attention, explain to them what they would be devouring upon if they chose this, and simply have their mouths watering.

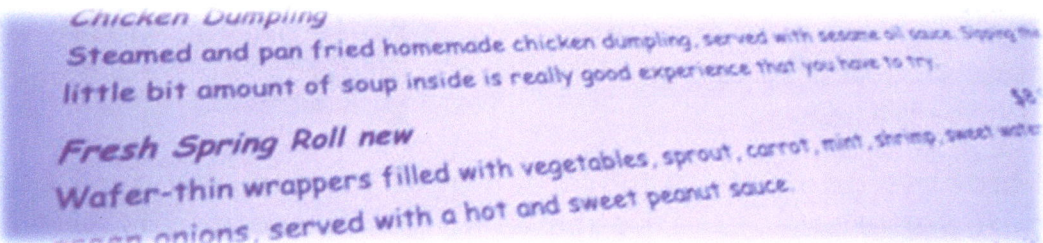

Here's how you should go about writing your menu descriptions:

1. **Find the Balance**
   You need to find the perfect balance. Both too little information and too much information are bad. Usually, it is a great idea to list only the major ingredients along with their cooking methods. You may also want to include the origins of a particular product. In some cases, the size of the portion should also be included in the description.

2. **Choose Format for the Menu Description**
   Generally, there are two types of format that you can choose:
   - i)   Heading along with a description; or
   - ii)   Heading as the description

In the first type, you will have a heading that should include the name of the dish along with whatever base ingredient it contains, for example:

Cajun Chicken Pasta
A fine blend of creamy linguini tossed with sautéed chicken strips with delicious Cajun seasoning.

As for the second type, the whole heading would be a description as follows:

Cajun chicken pasta with sautéed chicken strips tossed in creamy linguini and seasoned with Cajun.

3. Avoid Confusing the Customers

Every attempt should be made to ensure that there is nothing in the menu that would confuse the customers. This means no use of slang or abbreviations. For example, you should avoid:

- Writing w/ instead of 'with'; or
- Veggies instead of 'vegetables'

4. Avoid Spelling Mistakes

One of the worst things that you can do to give off a bad impression of your restaurant is by not checking for or correcting spelling mistakes. Do not think even for a moment that customers won't notice – more people notice mistakes than you can imagine; and if you run a fine-dining restaurant, it will be noticed more!

4.6 Be Truthful – Always

Being truthful is important not just because it's nice to speak the truth, but because it is the law. The Federal Government's Food, Drug and Cosmetic Act of 1938 prohibit any kind of representation, be it in written form or a pictorial form, which misrepresents the actual item.

You should serve an item exactly the way it is represented on the menu – not doing so could put your restaurant in a compromising position and make you liable for fraud.

Make sure that the following items are represented truthfully:

- Product Quantity

- Product Quality
- Product Price
- Points of Origin of Ingredients
- Product Preparation Techniques
- Nutritional Values, if any

4.7 Help Customers Make the Choice

With so many choices on the menu, customers can have a really hard time making up their minds. By helping your customers choose, you'll be improving not only your customer service, but you would also be increasing your sales as a result.

Here's how you can help your customers in choosing what to order:

- **Design a Simple Menu –** We have already discussed many ideas that can help you design a menu that could help by increasing your profit. Nonetheless, whichever approach you decide to take, the menu should be simple enough for customers to understand. If you include too many items on the menu, then ultimately the customers will be overwhelmed and that would render them unable to make the selection. On the other hand, having too many items will also add to your restaurant's expenses as you will need to keep all the required items in stock, in case a customer decides to try one of your least popular dishes!

- **Categorize the Choices –** All items in your menu should be categorized. How you categorize them is up to you. You could categorize based on a particular part of the world where the dish comes from, or you could divide the items based on what type of meat they contain and so on.

  The whole point of categorizing the items is to help you customers locate the items in a quick and convenient manner. If they are in the mood for having chicken, they can simply skip everything and proceed to where it says Chicken – simple, isn't it?

- **Group Same Items Together –** A great way to enhance your menu and make it more useful is by grouping together items that are usually purchased together. For example, a fast food chain main want to list burgers, fries and cold drinks closer together. This method has also proven to increase sales as people are tempted to order more – especially when they are hungry!

- **Offer Recommendations –** Some customers simply have no idea on what they should order. Some are bad decision makers and they rely on others to help them choose and make decisions for them. In this case, you can give them a shoulder by offering them recommendations. Recommendations can be printed on the menu, but there's a way with some added personal touch. Have your server make them a recommendation – something that is perhaps Chef's special for the day.

A word of caution though, having a simple menu doesn't mean you can leave it as it is for years to come. You need to cater for the changing needs of your customers and also consider adding more choices with time. A new item on the menu is always a highlight that usually doesn't go unnoticed.

4.8 Use Local Foods

A lot of people have become quite health conscious over time and they are making healthier choices when it comes to food. You can capitalize on this by offering fresh, local foods that don't have to travel great distances before they are consumed. Using local foods is becoming the trend of today as everyone from simple cafés to fine-dining restaurants are using them in their dishes.

Here's why you should seriously consider getting local foods from a farm nearby:

- They are fresh, *really* fresh – Fruits and vegetables in the United States have to commute –on average- around 1500 miles before they reach a place of their consumption. These are the commercially grown harvest that has been engineered precisely so that they can endure the long commutes. Fresh produce will become stale over such long distances.
  This is why by utilizing local foods, you'll be offering the freshest produce to your customers, and you can use it to proudly market your restaurant!

- **They taste better –** Because they are fresh from the farm, they have a taste far better than that of the commercially grown produce. If you have a knack for gardening, you'll agree with this point – nothing tastes better and fresher than the vegetables from your own garden.
- **They Support Local Economy –** You can support your local economy by purchasing the produce from your local markets. This will also help you build relations in the local community and also contribute to increased sales.

- **They Market Well -** Nothing is better for marketing than adding terms like *farm fresh* or *fresh from the farm*. No one complains about fresh food!
- **They Offer Flexible Menus –** The local produce varies depending on the seasons, and this offers restaurant owners a great opportunity to rotate their menus. This is great as it will keep your customers curious as to what you'll be offering in the coming season.
- **They Aren't Limited to Just Vegetables and Fruits –** It is a common misconception that you can only get vegetables and fruits in their respective seasons. Local foods also include poultry, beef as well as dairy products.
- **They Offer More Variety –** There are numerous types of produce that only local farms can offer you. These vegetables or fruits are not suited for commercial farming and you can use these unique produce to add more flavor to your food.

All these reasons make local foods an excellent option for you. Not only you'll be offering a healthy alternative, but you'll also have a chance to earn more by increasing your sales!

4.9 Offer Cuisines From Around The World

You can expand your menu's offering by introducing numerous types of cuisines from around the world. People love trying out different dishes from around the world. Here are some types of cuisines that you can offer:

1. Italian	6. Thai
2. Mexican	7. French
3. Japanese	8. Mediterranean
4. Indian	9. Lebanese
5. Chinese	10. Turkish

You don't have to offer more than one type of cuisine if you don't want to; specializing in a single type of cuisine is sometimes a good idea.

4.10 Avoid Deadly Mistakes on a Restaurant Menu

Finally, to sum up on the topic of menu design, there are some mistakes that you must avoid at all costs.

1. **Hand-Written Alterations** – Some restaurants, in an attempt to save the meager costs of digital printing, perform hand-written alterations on the menu. Not only does this look unprofessional, it also portrays a non-serious attitude towards customer care.

2. **Incorrectly Spelled Items** – Careful attention and time needs to be given to proof read the menu before the final copies are printed. If you have designed the menu yourself, then you need to ask someone to go through the menu for you in order to spot any mistakes that you may have missed.

3. **Listing Items That Are Not Available** – Another thing to avoid is to list any items that are not available regularly. Some restaurants fail to remove items that they have stopped offering altogether.

4. **Too Many Or Too Few Items** – As we have previously discussed, too many choices can end up confusing your customers. Whereas, too few items may cause the customers to leave if they cannot find anything of their liking.

5. **Frequent Changes** – Your regular customers would generally order the regular things that they have at your place. If you remove those items because of frequent changes in the menu, you are sure to disappoint them.

6. **Poor Design** – Not utilizing the principles of menu psychology in designing your menu can result in difficulties for the customers. The overall design of your menu should complement the theme of your restaurant and should be appealing and attractive to the eye.

5 MOTIVATING YOUR STAFF

The success of a business depends largely on how successful you have been in keeping your customers satisfied. This is why, for years, customer satisfaction has been every business's number one priority. However, during the pursuit of success, a lot of managers have forgotten the importance of a happy workforce. The happiness of the employees directly affects their productivity and performance – all your efforts can be wiped out by a single unhappy employee. Hiring employees and training them will cost you, and it could also affect the overall sales of your restaurant due to a lack of efficient workforce.

This is why it makes it essential that managers take causal steps in order to ensure that their team is well-motivated and happy. There are several reasons as to why you should keep your employees happy, and they are as follows:

Employee Retention

Every entrepreneur knows how expensive and time consuming it can be to hire new people and to provide them with the essential training. Unless an employee has become a liability to the company, it is best to retain the employee. Employee retention is only possible by keeping the employees happy, otherwise, people will move on the moment they get a better opportunity elsewhere.

It Affects Customer Service

Have you ever been to a place where the employees were disgruntled? It showed from the way they behaved, didn't it?

That's the last thing you would want for your restaurant – a disgruntled, de-motivated and unhappy employee can ruin the whole concept of good customer service.

Employee Performance

According to a study by the Kansas State University in 2009, happy employees perform to the best of their abilities and work in extremely efficient ways. This is exactly what you need to aim for as a restaurant owner. Greater efficiency translates into greater income – no catch here!

Greater Profit

When the employees are happy and working at their peak efficiency levels, they make fewer mistakes and perform their duties well within time. These employees can also go a long way in protecting the business's assets and safeguarding them against harm.

This section will offer you ideas on how to motivate your employees and keep them happy!

5.1 Set an Example

Quite often, people look up to people for guidance and as a restaurant owner and a manager, the person who they should look up to should be you. You have to set a positive example for them which they could follow. If you lack professionalism, you wouldn't be much of an example, would you?

Here are a few things you should do to set a good example for your team:

- Ensure that you carry a positive attitude at all times.
- Make sure you come to work on time, just like you would expect your team members to do and accomplish as many tasks as you can.
- If you have created policies and rules for your workplace, you need to be certain that you are following them too. There should be no exceptions when it comes to set rules.
- Never make unethical choices; otherwise you would be setting a precedent for your employees.
- Your approach towards problems at work should be proactive.
- Work with your employees towards new challenges and overcome obstacles with them – lead well, and they will follow.

5·2 Communicate With Your Employees

Communication with your employees is vital to the success of your business. Being a business owner doesn't mean you can simply leave this part to the manager – sometimes it's better to avoid creating a hierarchical structure. By communicating directly with the employees, you will make them feel valued and respected.

Good communication culture doesn't develop on its own; it needs to be established.

Establish the Culture

The first and foremost thing that you need to do is to be as transparent as possible with your employees. This includes each and everything from your business plan to the financial status of the company. Being transparent will give birth to a bond of trust between you and your workforce.

An HR consultant from Illinois once said: "*Your employees know you make more money than they do.*"

"What they don't understand is that you take more risk. They won't be able to understand the risk until they understand the business."

This is why you need to *help* them understand the business so that they know what risks are involved – remember that they constitute *your* team.

Arrange One on One Meetings

Apart from holding meetings with all of your staff, you should also consider setting up one on one meeting with each of your employees with the aim of just getting to know them better. This sort of a meeting can be a really powerful motivational tool. You could also discuss each of your employee's performance in a constructive manner without being harsh in anyway.

5·3   Keep an Open Ear

Always keep an ear open to feedback and queries from your employees. They may offer you ideas or suggestions on particulars that could help improve sales. By providing a kind of a platform for them, you will be instilling into them a sense of ownership.

Feedback Methods

Here are ways to get feedback from your employees:

Conduct a Survey

A full scale survey is a great way to get feedback from your employees. You could regularly carry out surveys that will offer your employees a chance to anonymously give out feedback

and suggestions. However, don't make a habit of throwing a survey onto your employees on a regular basis, as this could make them lose interest.

Place a Comment Box

A comment box doesn't have to be only for your customers – place a box especially for your employees who can drop off feedback whenever they want to. While it may seem as being an ancient way of asking for suggestions, it will send out a general message that you are always open to suggestions besides the surveys.

Ensuring Maximum Participation

Typical response rates of employee surveys linger between 70 to 90 percent. To further encourage participation, try out the following ways:

- Offer Anonymity – Some employees may not be entirely comfortable in disclosing their identity along with the feedback. Offer them an option to remain anonymous and you will see response rates rise!
- Encourage – Encouragement from the management is necessary to fuel higher response rates. This can be done by sending out reminders to all employees requesting them to participate and provide feedback for the betterment of the restaurant.
- Offer Incentives – Offering incentives to those who provide feedback in any form is another way of increasing the response rates. However, incentives have been known to reduce the accuracy of the feedback in a few cases.

5.4 Appraise and Praise

The importance of a fair performance appraisal system cannot be undermined. A performance appraisal system offers great benefits and helps a business retain its employees.

You should also consider implementing an appraisal system in your restaurant where you could analyze their performance over a couple of months and offer pay raises and other incentives – based on how well they performed.

Performance Appraisal Systems can provide:

Objectives

An appraisal system can provide an employee with goals and objectives that he or she needs to meet during the period until the next appraisal evaluation. It also provides them a chance to take an overview on how well they had been performing, their strengths and weaknesses and how they can go about improving their output.

Career Development

An appraisal system also helps an employee by offering pay raises, promotions and numerous other things that could be classified under career development. Who would want to work for years with the same pay and benefits, and zero promotion?

Good performance should always be praised lavishly. For an employee, pay isn't everything – a word of praise from the boss can go a long way in keeping them motivated and will make them feel that their good work is being noticed.

5·5 Set Daily Targets

Another great way to increase productivity while giving the employees something to look forward to is by setting daily sale targets. For example, you could have daily competitions of whoever serves the most customers would become eligible for a bonus at the end of the day.

The bonus could be in any number of forms, ranging from gift cards, cash prizes, gifts and perhaps even a paid leave for a day!

5·6 Set Monthly Sales Targets

Similar to the daily targets, you could also consider setting monthly sales targets for the employees. By giving a specific target to your workforce, you give them something to aim for.

While setting the goals, you should ensure that:

- The goals and targets fall within your restaurant's business strategy
- The targets must be clear and easy to understand by everyone

on your team
- Each and every member of the staff should understand their importance as it is they who will be implementing them
- The set targets must be practical and achievable, yet challenging
- The rewards should also be clearly mentioned

5.7 Enforce Respect and Equality

This is one thing where even the slightest of deviation should not be tolerated. You must ensure that the working environment at your restaurant is such that each and every member of your staff is treated with utmost respect and equality –regardless of their race, color or creed!

If they make a mistake, that still gives no one the right to be disrespectful. Every other employee at the restaurant, regardless of their position, should follow these guidelines:

- Never, ever insult anyone by calling them names or putting them down
- Everyone should treat each other with the due respect, regardless of their race, religion, gender, size, country of organ or age.
- Criticism should be kept to a minimum; and if required, only constructive criticism should be offered – that too in a way that would not belittle anyone.

Implement the idea that every employee should 'Treat others as they wish to be treated'.

5·8 Show Appreciation

Appreciation is the number one factor that motivates employees. Appreciate good performance of your employees in the following ways:

- Praise good work that is done by an employee so that they know their hard work is being noted.
- A simple *thank you* to a person can make them feel valued and appreciated. Thank your employees for working hard.
- Get to know your staff on a personal level – this doesn't count as being nosy. On the contrary, they will feel that they are cared for and respected.
- Surprise hard working individuals with a random gift
- Everyone loves food – offer your employees free dinner with their families

5·9 Provide Training

By providing regular training sessions, you'll not only be improving the capabilities of your staff, but you'll also be instilling in them a sense of purpose and opportunity for growth.

There are several methods through which you can impart training to your staff.

Training by Demonstration

A demonstration can be carried out by an instructor while trainees observe and learn, similar to popular cooking shows.

Training by Shadowing

Shadowing is a more personal type of demonstration. Trainees can follow their mentor while

he or she performs the daily duties. This method allows a more hands-on type of learning experience.

Training by Instruction

In this method of training, a written and/or verbal instruction is provided to the trainees without any actual demonstration. This is how most classrooms work.

Training by Supervised Performance

This method allows the trainees to actually perform the duties while they are supervised, and thus allows the trainees to learn something while they do it themselves.

5·10 Provide a Fun Atmosphere

Who wouldn't love a place that is fun to work at? Add some fun to your restaurant and ease off tension by implementing some humor.

For example, meetings don't have to be all formal where everyone is as tense as a bamboo stick. Try throwing candies around to ease off the tension in the environment.

Offer fun incentives and eat together during breaks while sharing jokes with your staff – a workplace doesn't need to be serious all the time, a light atmosphere can actually boost productivity by eliminating stress for good.

If you can't think of anything else, ask your employees for ideas – make smile compulsory!

CONCLUSION

The best thing about running a business in the hospitality industry is the versatility. Most of the time, there are no hard and fast rules that have to be followed. The possibilities are endless; and as a restaurant owner, you'll agree that gaining an edge over competition is not as difficult provided that you unleash your imagination and creativity and reach out to your customers.

The traditional marketing tactics have changed since the inception of the digital age, and using technology, restaurant owners now have a greater chance increasing their bottom line.

The ideas that have been presented in this book are bound to help you transform your restaurant in a way that adheres to today's modern hospitality industry standards.

After all, owning a restaurant is among one of the greatest types of businesses a person can have – and now you have the ability to boost your sales along with heading in a direction that will take your business to new heights of success. Wishing you all the best...